ROAD TO DAMASCUS

Activity Book for Beginners

Road to Damascus Activity Book for Beginners

Bible Pathway Adventures® is a trademark of BPA Publishing Ltd.
Defenders of the Faith® is a trademark of BPA Publishing Ltd.

ISBN: 978-1-7772168-0-1

Author: Pip Reid
Creative Director: Curtis Reid

For free Bible resources including coloring pages, worksheets, puzzles and more, visit our website at:

www.biblepathwayadventures.com

Introduction for Parents

Enjoy teaching your children about the Bible with our *Road to Damascus Activity Book for Beginners*. Packed with lesson plans, worksheets, coloring pages, and puzzles to help educators just like you teach children a Biblical faith. Includes scripture references for easy Bible verse look-up and a handy answer key for teachers.

Bible Pathway Adventures helps educators teach children a Biblical faith in a fun and creative way. We do this via our Activity Books and free printable activities – available on our website: www.biblepathwayadventures.com

Thanks for buying this Activity Book and supporting our ministry. Every book purchased helps us continue our work providing free Classroom Packs and discipleship resources to families and missions around the world.

The search for Truth is more fun than Tradition!

Table of Contents

LESSON 1 | Lesson Plan
Saul, Stephen, and the disciples

Teacher: _____

Today's Bible passage: Acts 7:54-60

Welcome prayer:
Pray a simple prayer with the children before you begin the lesson.

Lesson objectives:
In this lesson, children will learn:
1. The character of Stephen
2. Why the religious leaders had Stephen killed

Did You Know?
Paul was Saul's Roman name. Sha'ul (or Saul) was his Hebrew name.

Bible lesson overview:
In Jerusalem, men called disciples talked to the people about Yeshua (Jesus). One disciple was a man named Stephen. He was strong and full of courage. Because the religious leaders did not believe that Yeshua was the Messiah, they did not like Stephen. A group of men took him outside the city gate. There, they gave their coats to a man named Saul, and started throwing stones at Stephen. Stephen fell on his knees and prayed, "God, do not blame them for doing this!" These were the last words Stephen spoke before he died.

Let's Review:

Questions to ask your students:

1. Who was Stephen?
2. Why did the religious leaders not like Stephen?
3. Where did the men take Stephen?
4. Who did the men give their coats to?
5. What did the men do to Stephen?

 A memory verse to help children remember God's Word:

"Stephen was full of the Holy Spirit." (Acts 7:55)

 ## Activities:

Coloring page: Saul

Worksheet: Angry men

Worksheet: Trace the Words

Connect the dots: A religious leader

Worksheet: Tzitzits

Worksheet: What a lot of coats!

Alphabet worksheets: C is for coat

Bible activity: Stoning of Stephen

Worksheet: Stephen was brave!

Bible word search puzzle: Stoning of Stephen

 ## Closing prayer:

End the lesson with a small prayer.

Saul (Paul)

Saul was a religious leader. His job was to teach people about God. Trace the letters. Color the picture.

Saul

🌿 Angry men 🌿

A group of men were angry with Stephen.
They did not like him teaching people about the Messiah.
Circle and color the angry faces.

🍃 Trace the Words 🍃

Color the pictures.

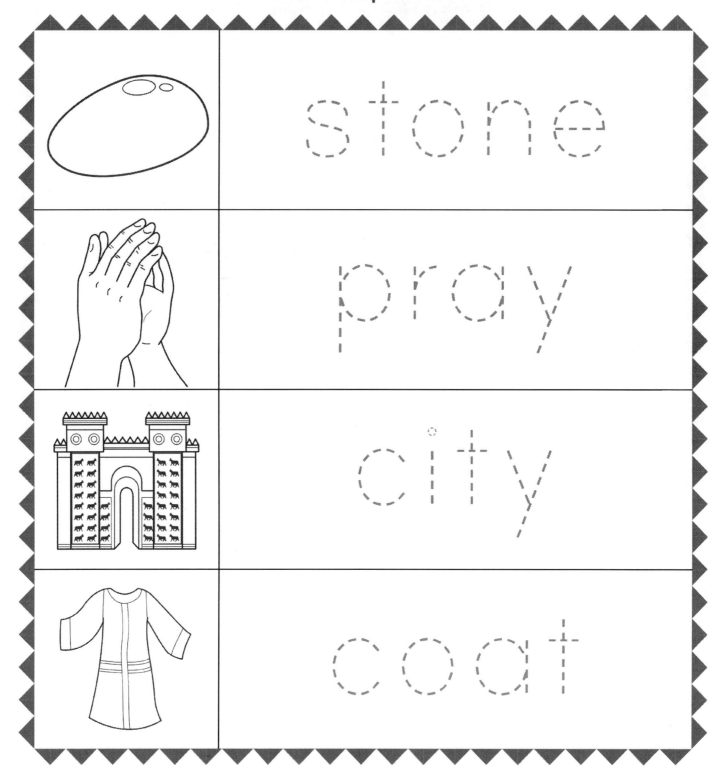

A religious leader

Saul was a religious leader. Many religious leaders did not like Stephen. Connect the dots to see the picture.

Tzitzits

At the time of Saul, Israelite men wore tassels on their clothes to help them remember God's commandments (Deuteronomy 22:12).
These tassels are called tzitzits.

Color and trace the set of tzitzits below.

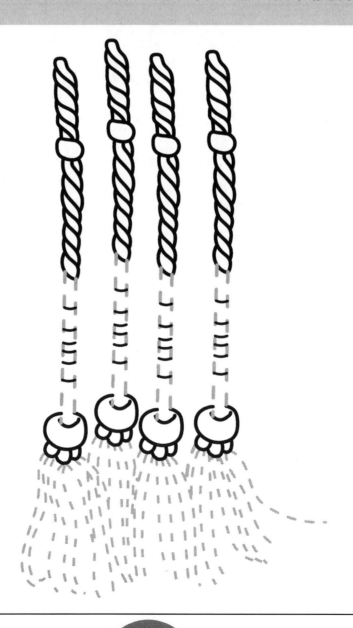

What a lot of coats!

Saul took care of the men's coats while they stoned Stephen. Count the coats and write the number in the box.

🌿 C is for Coat 🌿

Saul took care of the men's coats. (Acts 7:58).
Trace the letters. Color the picture.

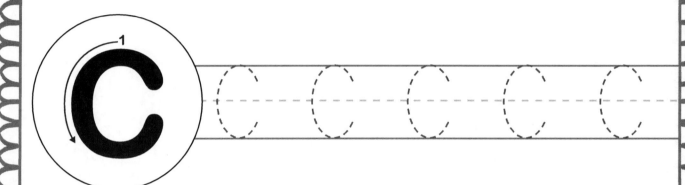

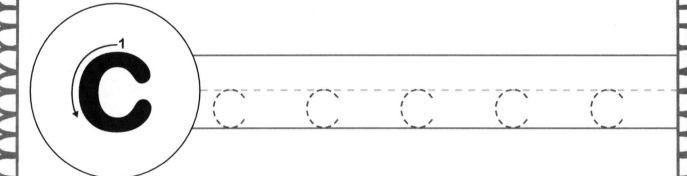

Trace the letter c

Color the coat

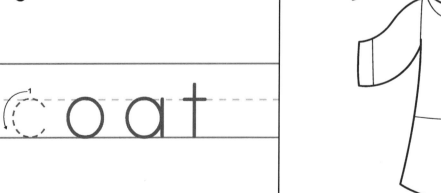

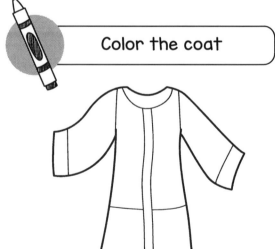

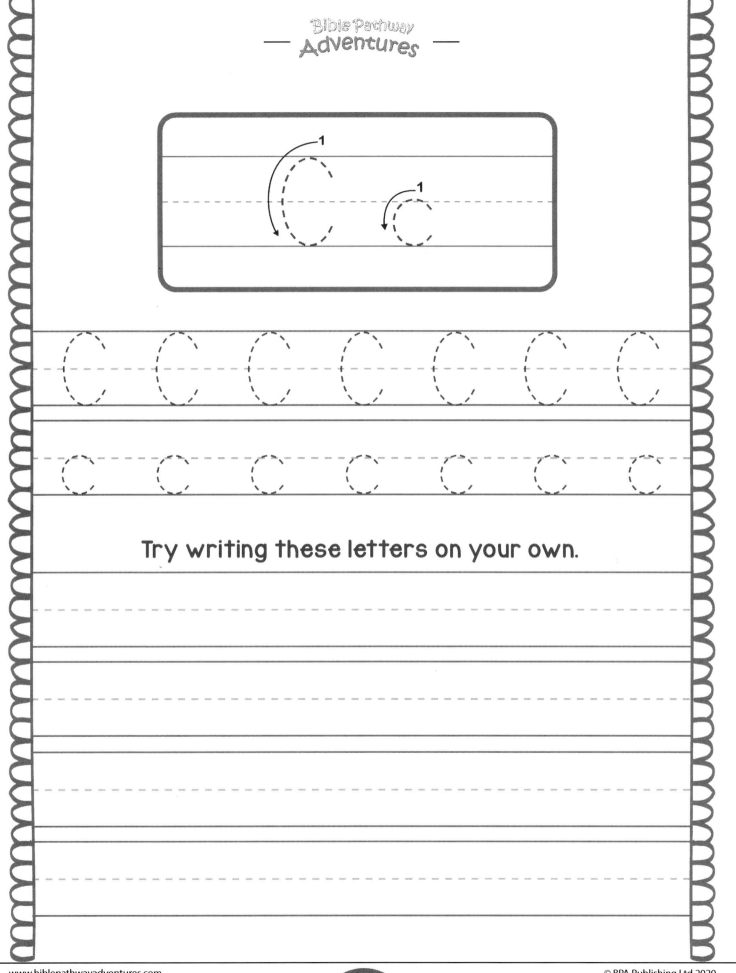

Try writing these letters on your own.

✿ Stephen was brave! ✿

Stephen was brave. Being brave is doing the right thing even when it is hard. Think about a time you were brave. Draw yourself doing something brave in the bubble below.

🌿 Stoning of Stephen 🌿

Find and circle each of the words from the list below.

```
P F P M S C
Y R C E T I
Q T A N O T
J G C Y N Y
S A U L E K
B R A V E B
```

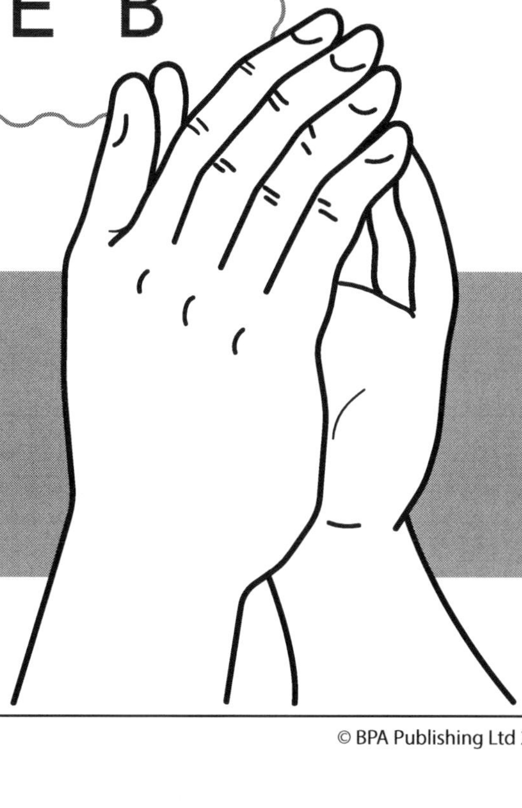

MEN   STONE

SAUL   BRAVE

CITY   PRAY

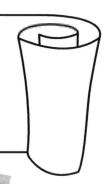

LESSON 2 | Lesson Plan
Road to Damascus

Teacher: _____

Today's Bible passage: Acts 9:1-9

Welcome prayer:
Pray a simple prayer with the children before you begin the lesson.

Lesson objectives:
In this lesson, children will learn:
1. Why Saul went to Damascus
2. What happened to Saul on the road to Damascus

Did You Know?
A synagogue is a building. It is also a meeting place where people gather.

Bible lesson overview:
Saul did not like people speaking about Yeshua the Messiah. He wanted to stop them as fast as possible! The High Priest gave Saul permission to go to the city of Damascus. There, he planned to find people who believed in Yeshua. Near Damascus, a bright light shone from heaven. Saul fell to the ground. A voice said to him, "Saul, why are you persecuting Me?" Saul did not know who it was. "Who are you?" he asked. The voice said, "I am Yeshua. Go into the city. Someone will tell you what to do." But Saul could not see anything. He was blind! His friends took him into the city where he did not eat or drink for three days.

Let's Review:

Questions to ask your students:

1. Why did Saul want to go to Damascus?
2. Who gave Saul permission to go to Damascus?
3. What did Saul do when he saw a bright light?
4. Who spoke to Saul?
5. How long did Saul not eat or drink?

 A memory verse to help children remember God's Word:

"Saul could not see for three days." (Acts 9:9)

 ## Activities:

Worksheet: The high priest
Worksheet: Duties of a high priest
Worksheet: Road to Damascus
Bible activity: Road to Damascus
Maze: Road to Damascus
Worksheet: What can you hear?
Worksheet: A light from heaven
Worksheet: L is for light
Worksheet: How do you see?
Worksheet: The number three
Worksheet: How long did Saul not eat?

 ## Closing prayer:

End the lesson with a small prayer.

🌿 The high priest 🌿

The high priest gave Saul letters to take to Damascus (Acts 9:1-2). Color the high priest's hat white. Color the robe blue.

🌿 Duties of a high priest 🌿

The high priest had many jobs. Can you name them?
Trace the words. Color the pictures.

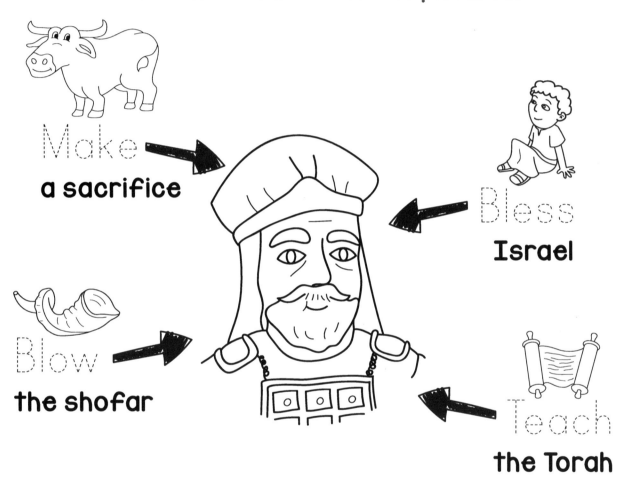

Make
a sacrifice

Bless
Israel

Blow
the shofar

Teach
the Torah

I see a high priest

Road to Damascus

Saul walked along a road to Damascus.
Trace the word 'road'. Circle and color the
pictures that start with the letter r.

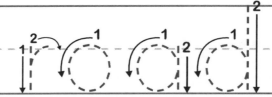

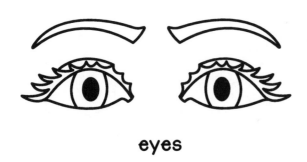

eyes

hair

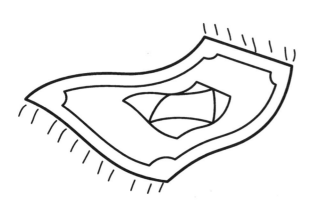

rug

rocket

Road to Damascus

After Saul met the high priest in Jerusalem, he went to Damascus (Acts 9:1-3). Help Saul get to Damascus.

🍃 What can you hear? 🍃

Saul heard a voice on the road to Damascus (Acts 9:4).
Color what you can hear.

baby

crown

shower

lion

birds

A light from heaven

Tear pieces of yellow tissue paper into small pieces.
Paste them into the empty space to show
the bright light. Color the picture of Saul.

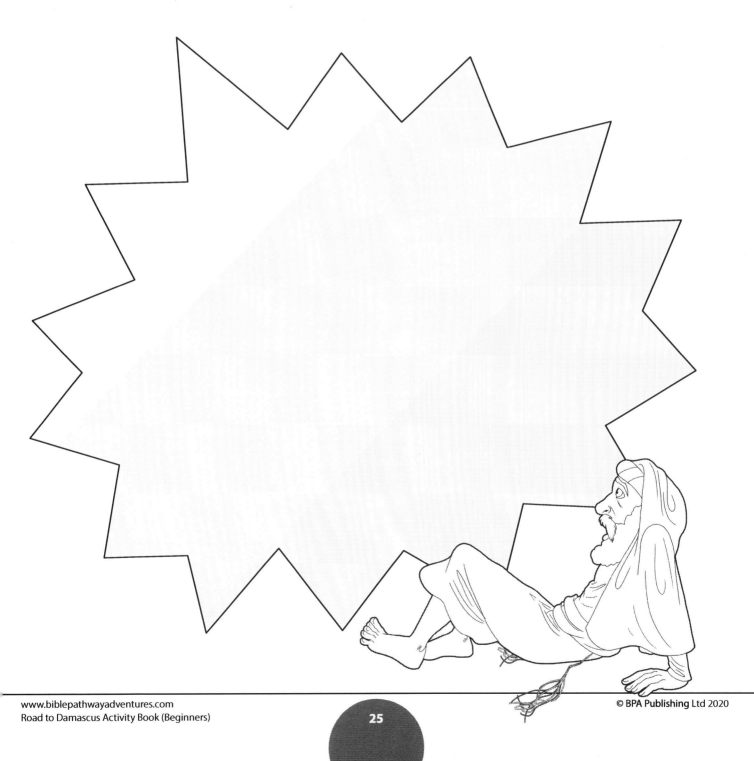

✳ L is for light ✳

is for

light

How do you see?

Our eyes help us to see things. On the road to Damascus, Saul opened his eyes but he could not see. He was blind! Match the words with the parts of an eye by tracing along the dotted lines.

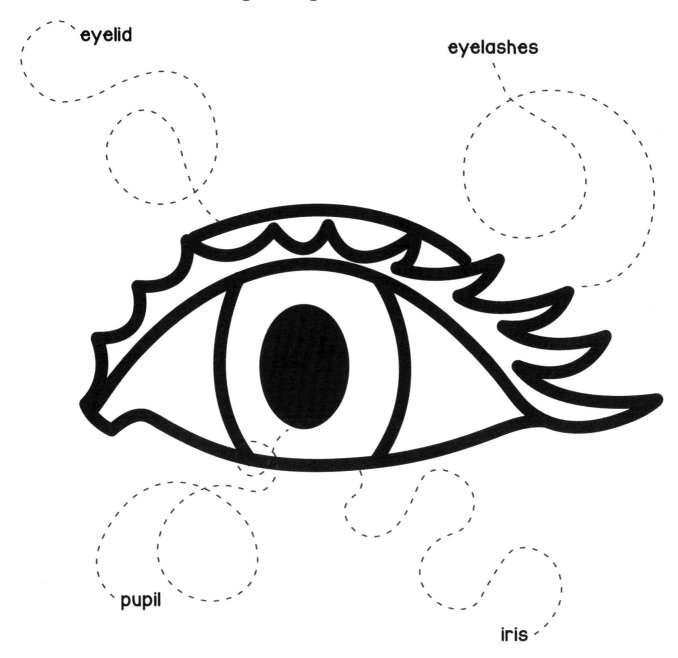

eyelid

eyelashes

pupil

iris

three

Saul could not see for three days.

Write the number three in the boxes below.

How many fingers are there?

Whose voice did Saul hear on the road to Damascus?

....

How long did Saul not eat?

Fill in the blanks using the chart below.

Can you read the sentence?

$\overline{}$ $\overline{}$ $\overline{}$ $\overline{}$ $\overline{}$ $\overline{}$ $\overline{}$ $\overline{}$ $\overline{}$

20 8 18 5 5   4 1 25 19

A	B	C	D	E	F	G	H	I	J	K	L	M
1	2	3	4	5	6	7	8	9	10	11	12	13

N	O	P	Q	R	S	T	U	V	W	X	Y	Z
14	15	16	17	18	19	20	21	22	23	24	25	26

LESSON 3 | Lesson Plan
Escape from Damascus

Teacher: _____

Today's Bible passage: Acts 9:10-25

Welcome prayer:
Pray a simple prayer with the children before you begin the lesson.

Lesson objectives:
In this lesson, children will learn:
1. What Saul did while he stayed in Damascus
2. How Saul escaped from Damascus

Did You Know?
Damascus is the oldest city in the world. People have lived there for more than 5000 years.

Bible lesson overview:
A man named Ananias went to Saul. He put his hands on Saul's eyes. Suddenly, Saul could see again! He stood up and washed himself in a special bath called a mikveh. Then, he began teaching people about the Messiah. Many people listened to him and believed what he said. But a group of men did not like Saul, and wanted to kill him. Luckily, Saul's disciples heard about their plan. They had an idea! They put Saul in a basket and lowered him down the city wall. Saul had escaped Damascus!

Let's Review:

Questions to ask your students:

1. Who put his hands on Saul's eyes?
2. What did Saul do after he could see again?
3. Who did Saul talk to the people about?
4. Who wanted to kill Saul?
5. How did Saul escape the city?

 A memory verse to help children remember God's Word:

Saul said, "He is the son of God." (Acts 9:20)

Activities:

Worksheet: What is a mikveh?

Coloring page: Ananias visits Saul

Let's learn Hebrew: Sha'ul

Worksheet: I spy!

Bible flashcards: Saul

Bible craft: The great escape!

Worksheet: Who helped Saul escape?

Worksheet: The number one

Worksheet: Day and night

Worksheet: To Jerusalem

Worksheet: Let's move!

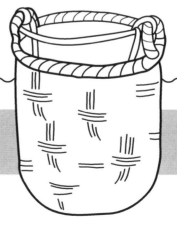

 Closing prayer:

End the lesson with a small prayer.

🌿 What is a mikveh? 🌿

A mikveh is a pool of water or bath. When Saul was alive, many houses had a mikveh. Men and women cleaned themselves in a mikveh after a special event. Color the water inside the mikveh.

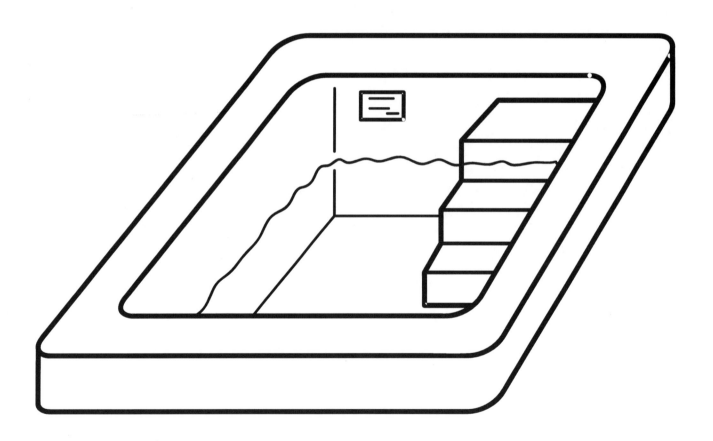

🌿 Ananias visits Saul 🌿

God told Ananias to go and see Saul.
Draw Ananias to finish the drawing.

✷ Sha'ul ✷

Paul had two names. His Hebrew name
was Sha'ul and his Greek name was Paul.

Sha'ul

שָׁאוּל

Paul

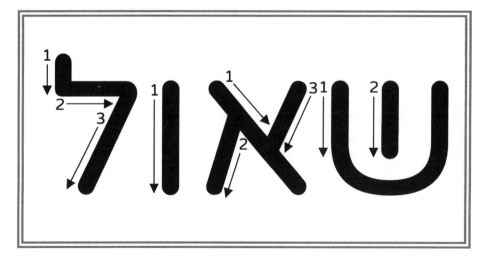

Let's write!

Practice writing Paul's Hebrew name on the lines below.

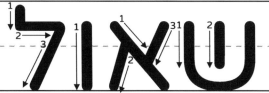

שָׁאוּל

Try this on your own.
Remember that Hebrew is read from RIGHT to LEFT.

🌿 I spy! 🌿

Saul escaped Damascus in a basket.
Color the same objects a single color. Then count each
type of object and write the number on the label.

Who helped Saul escape?

Trace along the ropes to find which disciple helped Saul.

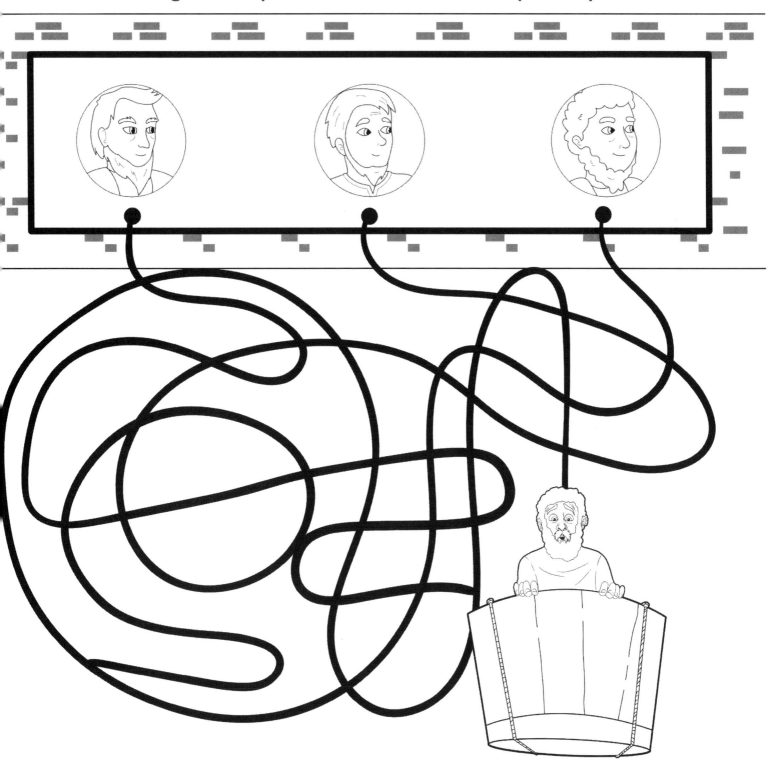

The number One

Saul escaped Damascus in a basket.
Write the number one. Color the one basket.

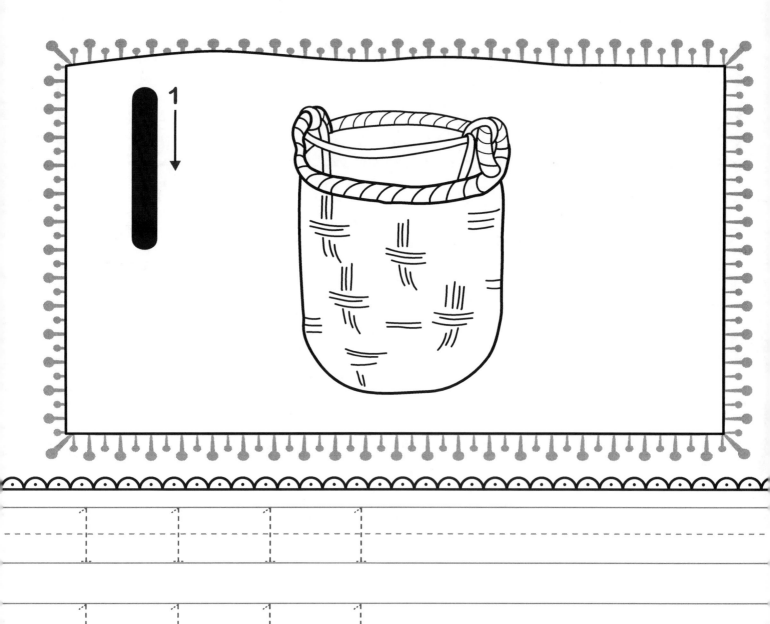

Day and night

Men watched the city gates day and night
to stop Saul escaping Damascus (Acts 9:24).
The moon shines at night. The sun shines in the day.

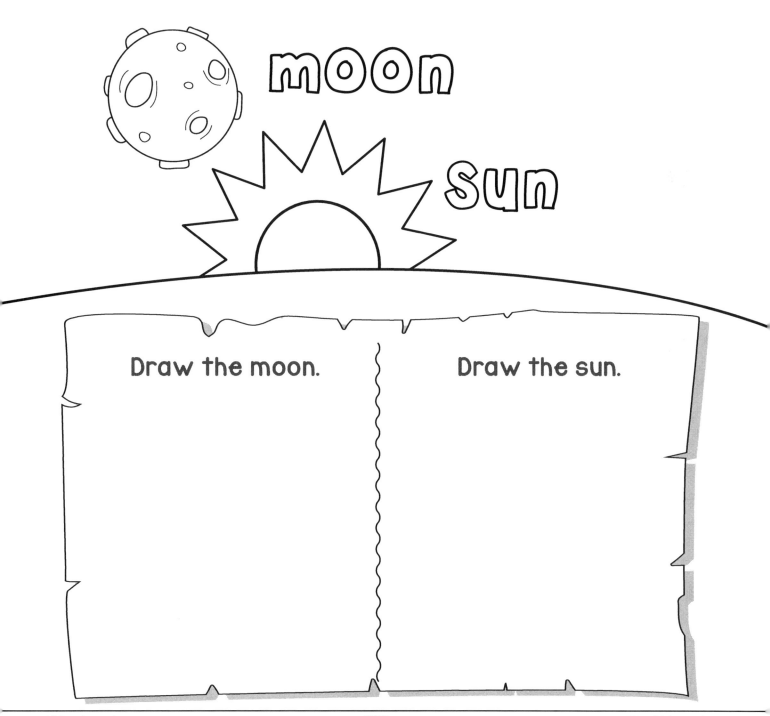

moon

sun

Draw the moon.

Draw the sun.

To Jerusalem...

Help Saul get from Damascus to Jerusalem
by coloring the letter j.

Let's move!

Saul moved from one place to another.
Color the objects that move.

flowers

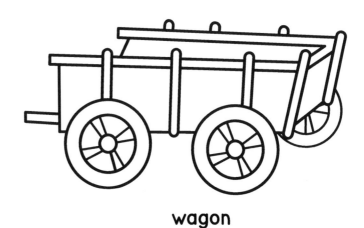

wagon

carrot

boat

raft

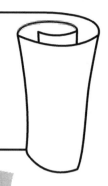

LESSON 4

Lesson Plan
Saul and the disciples

Teacher: _____

Today's Bible passage: Acts 9:26-29

Welcome prayer:
Pray a simple prayer with the children before you begin the lesson.

Lesson objectives:
In this lesson, children will learn:
1. Why the disciples were afraid of Saul
2. The character of Saul

Did You Know?
Saul was from the tribe of Benjamin, one of the twelve tribes of Israel.

Bible lesson overview:
After Saul escaped from Damascus, he went to Jerusalem. There, he tried to join the disciples. But they were afraid him. After all, Saul had tried to arrest their friends. A man named Barnabas took him to see the apostles. "Saul believes that Yeshua is the Messiah," he told them. After this, Saul spoke to many people about the Messiah. Some men in Jerusalem did not like Saul speaking to the people. They made plans to kill him.

Let's Review:

Questions to ask your students:

1. Why did Saul go to Jerusalem?
2. Why were the disciples were scared of Saul?
3. Who was Barnabas?
4. Use one word to describe Saul.
5. Why did some men want to kill Saul?

 A memory verse to help children remember God's Word:

"Saul went to Jerusalem." (Acts 9:26)

Activities:

Connect the dots: Saul

Worksheet: Saul goes to Jerusalem

Worksheet: A disciple

Coloring worksheet: Let's Draw

Worksheet: What's my sound?

Worksheet: D is for disciple

Worksheet: Label the disciple

Worksheet: Match the pictures

Worksheet: Wanted!

Worksheet: Courage

 Closing prayer:

End the lesson with a small prayer.

❧ Saul ❧

Connect the dots to see the picture.

Saul goes to Jerusalem

Imagine you are Saul. What items would you take with you to Jerusalem? Choose four items and draw them in the suitcase below.

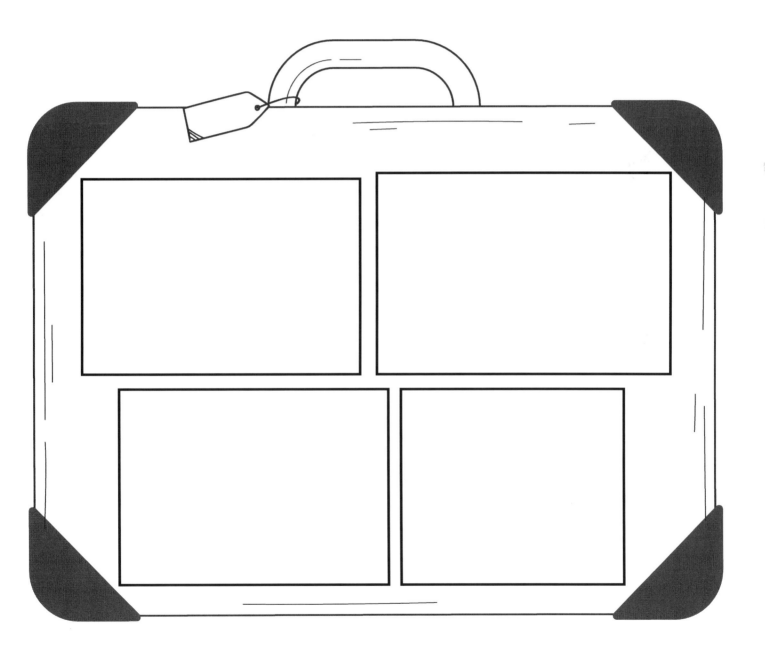

🌿 A disciple 🌿

A disciple is someone who follows Yeshua (Jesus)
and does what He says. Do you obey Yeshua?
Color part of the foot each day as you behave like Him.

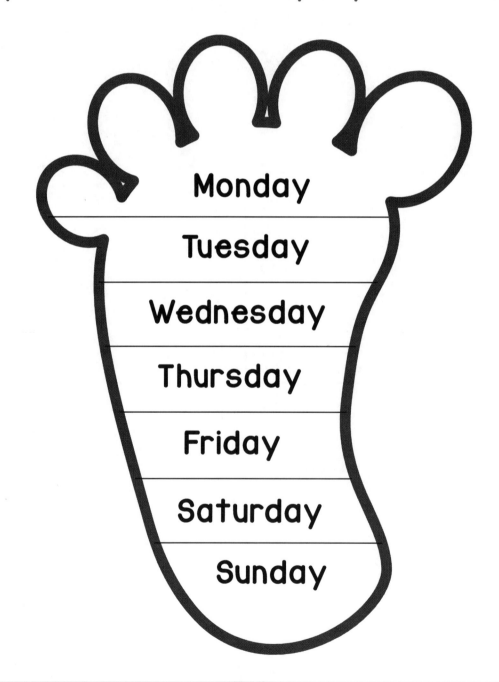

Monday

Tuesday

Wednesday

Thursday

Friday

Saturday

Sunday

Let's Draw!

In Jerusalem, Saul told the people about the Messiah (Acts 9:28). Draw Saul in Jerusalem.

What's my sound?

The disciples were afraid of Saul (Acts 9:26).
The word 'disciple' starts with the letter d. Circle and
color the pictures that start with the letter d.

dress

crown

deer

fox

lamp

D is for disciple

A disciple is someone who follows Yeshua (Jesus) and does what He says. Let's be the hands of Yeshua and love one another. Trace the words. Color the picture.

d disciple

D is for disciple

Label the disciple

The disciples wore different clothes to what you wear today. Use the words in the box to label parts of a disciple. Color the disciple.

sandals	tunic	hair	belt

🍃 Match the pictures 🍃

Draw a line to match the pictures with the sentences.
Color the pictures.

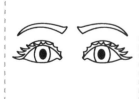

I see a basket.

I see a city.

I see eyes.

I see Saul.

WANTED

Name:...............................

COURAGE

Courage is doing something, even when you feel afraid. Some men did not like Saul speaking about the Messiah (Acts 9:28-29). They wanted to kill him. But Saul had courage. He still spoke boldly about Yeshua (Jesus).

Draw something I am afraid of.

Draw how I show courage.

LESSON 5 | Lesson Plan
Escape from Jerusalem

Teacher: _____

Today's Bible passage: Acts 9:29-30

Welcome prayer:
Pray a simple prayer with the children before you begin the lesson.

Lesson objectives:
In this lesson, children will learn:
1. Why Saul had to leave Jerusalem
2. Where the disciples sent Saul

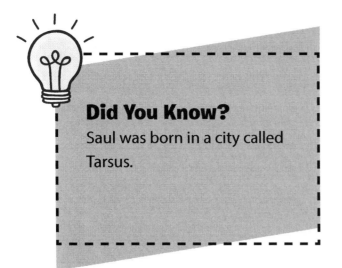

Did You Know?
Saul was born in a city called Tarsus.

Bible lesson overview:
Every day, Saul spoke to the people about the Messiah. But not everyone liked what Saul had to say. Some men made plans to kill him. When the disciples heard about their plans, they took Saul to a city by the sea called Caesarea. There, they put him on a boat and sent him to a faraway city called Tarsus. This was Saul's hometown. And from that time on, more and more people in the land of Israel began to believe in the Messiah.

Let's Review:

Questions to ask your students:

1. Where did Saul speak to the people about the Messiah?
2. What did some men in Jerusalem want to do to Saul?
3. Where did the disciples take Saul?
4. Where did the disciples send Saul?
5. What have you learned about Saul?

 A memory verse to help children remember God's Word:

"Saul spoke about the Messiah." (Acts 9:28)

Activities:

Worksheet: Good news!
Bible activity: The temple
Bible word search puzzle: Saul's escape!
Coloring page: Saul escapes Jerusalem
Worksheet: I can count!
Worksheet: Follow the path to Caesarea
Worksheet: The Romans
Map activity: Saul sails to Tarsus
Worksheet: Saul's hometown
Coloring page: God is with you
Worksheet: True or false?
Bible craft: Make a hanging mobile
Certificate of Award

 Closing prayer:

End the lesson with a small prayer.

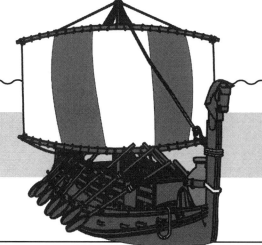

Good news!

Saul used his mouth to speak about the Messiah.
Trace the words. Color the pictures.

 I speak with my mouth

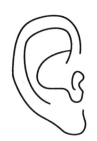 I hear with my ears

 I see with my eyes

 I pray with my hands

Saul's escape!

Find and circle each of the words from the list below.

```
S E A L C S
P Y U Y H P
L K Z M U E
C I T Y R A
R O A D C K
B O A T H C
```

SEA   CHURCH
BOAT   ROAD
CITY   SPEAK

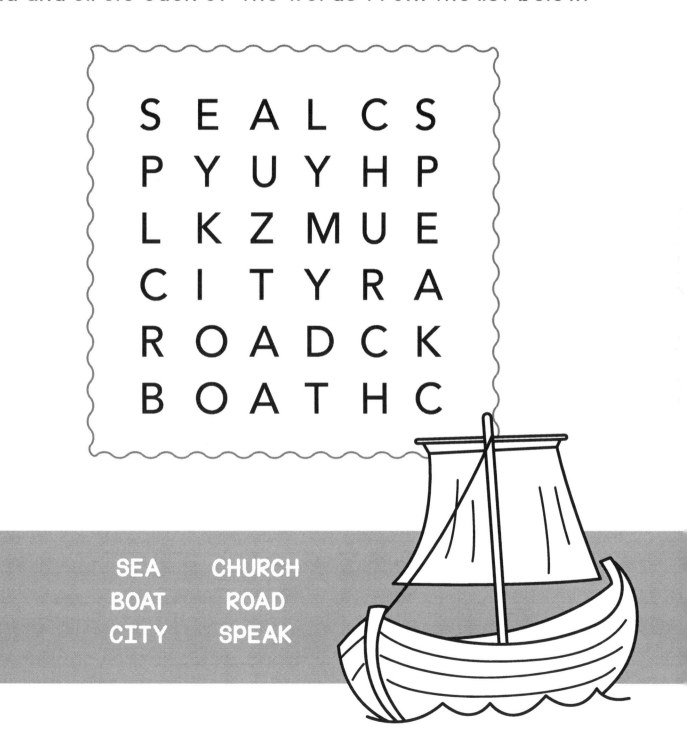

Saul escapes Jerusalem

To keep Saul safe, his friends took
him away from Jerusalem (Acts 9:30).
Draw Saul and the men escaping the city.

I can count!

Count the objects and write the number in the box.
Color the objects.

1   2   3   4   5   6

Follow the path to Caesarea

Let's learn the alphabet!
Help Saul and the disciples make their way
to Caesarea by following the path from A to Z.

🍃 The Romans 🍃

King Herod built the city of Caesarea.
He named the city after Caesar, the Roman Emperor.
Color the Roman coin.

🌿 Saul sails to Tarsus 🌿

Saul was born in a city called Tarsus. Connect the dots to help Saul get back to Tarsus.

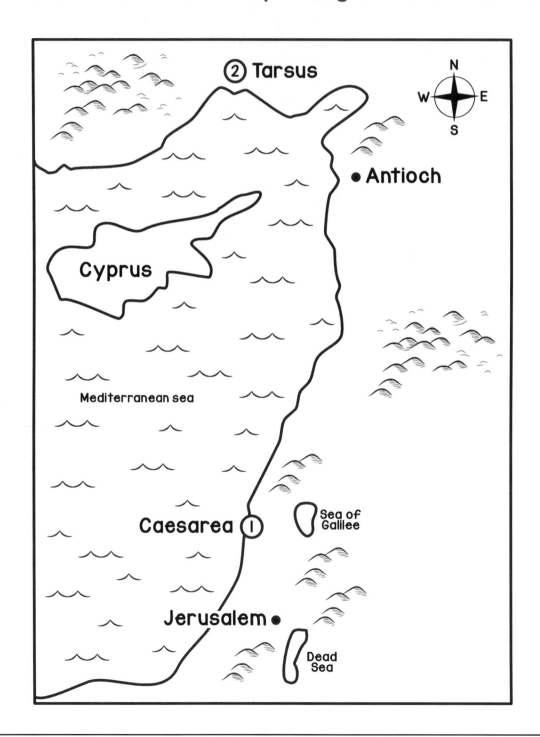

❧ Saul's hometown ❧

Saul was born in a city called Tarsus.
Trace the word 'Tarsus'. Circle and color the
pictures that start with the letter t.

Tarsus

tree

cow

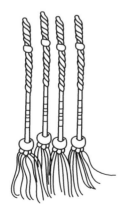

tzitzits

fire

"God is with you wherever you go."

(Joshua 1:9)

🌿 True or False? 🌿

Listen to the statements. Are they true or false?

Saul was a fireman.	Stephen was stoned to death.
Saul met Peter on the road to Damascus.	Saul escaped from Damascus.
Saul did not eat or drink for three days.	Saul lived in Egypt.

CRAFTS & PROJECTS

🌿 Stoning of Stephen 🌿

Color and cut out the people and objects.
Paste them outside the city.

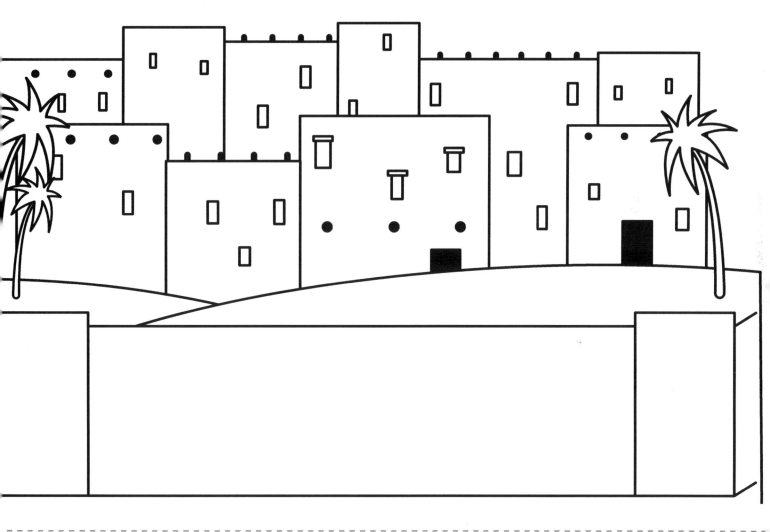

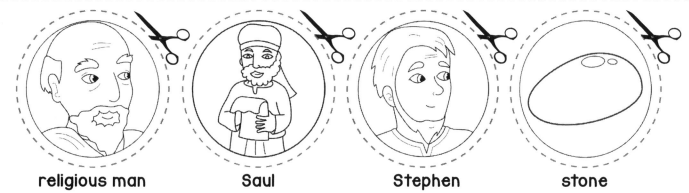

religious man   **Saul**   **Stephen**   **stone**

🌿 Road to Damascus 🌿

Saul and his friends went to Damascus to arrest followers
of the Messiah. Color and cut out the men and donkey.
Place them on the road.

Saul   donkey   friend   friend

Bible Pathway Adventures

🌿 Bible Flashcards 🌿

Color and cut out the flashcards.
Tape them around your home or classroom!

www.biblepathwayadventures.com
Road to Damascus Activity Book (Beginners)
© BPA Publishing Ltd 2020

priest

5

city

6

boat

7

coat

8

🌿 The great escape! 🌿

Help Saul escape Damascus by making him a basket.

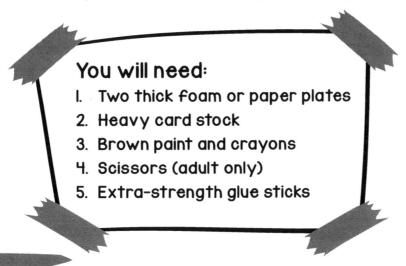

You will need:
1. Two thick foam or paper plates
2. Heavy card stock
3. Brown paint and crayons
4. Scissors (adult only)
5. Extra-strength glue sticks

Instructions:

1. Print the Saul template on the next page. Make a copy onto heavy card stock and cut out.
2. Cut one of the paper plates in half. Use the concave side for the front of the basket.
3. Make a handle by cutting another paper plate in half and leaving a handle around the edge. Glue the two sides together. Paint or color the paper plates brown.
4. While the paper plate is drying, ask the children to color Saul. When they have finished, place him in the basket.

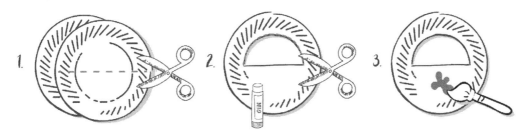

ta-da!

The Temple

There was a temple in Jerusalem. This is where the priests worked and people met to talk about God. Color and cut out the people. Place them in the temple.

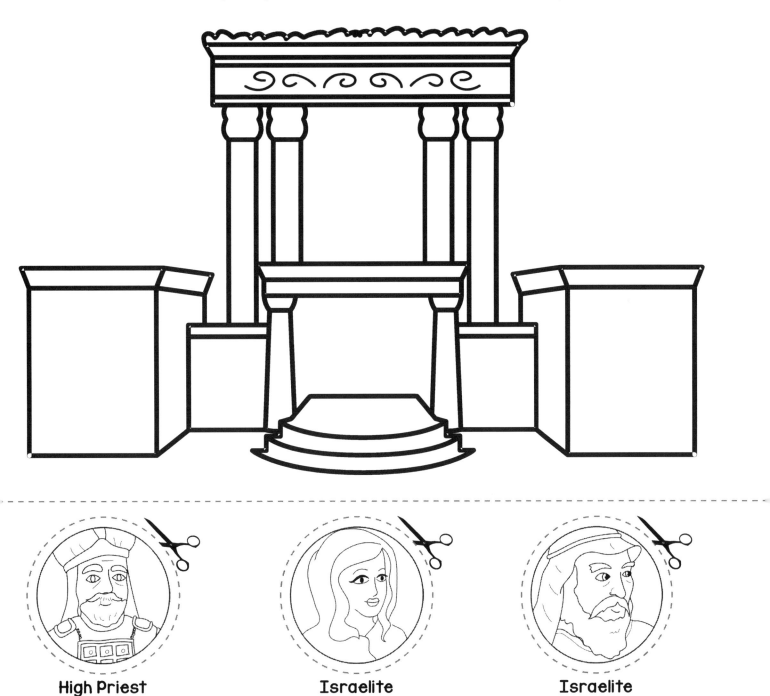

High Priest

Israelite

Israelite

❧ Make a hanging mobile ❧

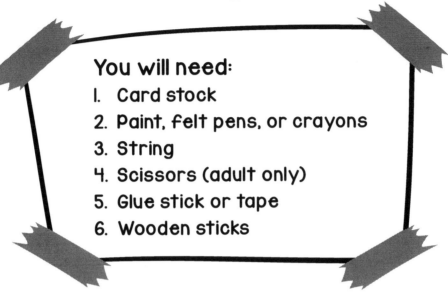

You will need:
1. Card stock
2. Paint, felt pens, or crayons
3. String
4. Scissors (adult only)
5. Glue stick or tape
6. Wooden sticks

Instructions:

1. Ask your child to color the pictures inside each circle.
2. When your child has finished coloring, cut out the mobile pieces and glue onto heavy card stock.
3. Make a hole at the top of each mobile piece, string the pieces together, and attach to a piece of wood.

1.

2.

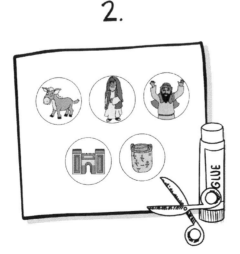

3.

ta-da!

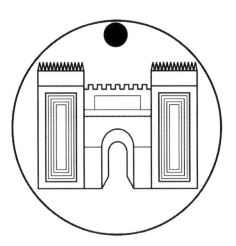
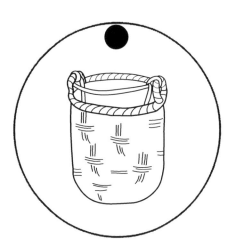

Certificate of Award

ANSWER KEY

LESSON ONE: Saul, Stephen, and the disciples
Let's Review answers:
1. A disciple
2. Stephen spoke about Yeshua the Messiah
3. Outside the city gate
4. Saul
5. The men threw stones at Stephen until he died

LESSON TWO: Road to Damascus
Let's Review answers:
1. Saul wanted to arrest some disciples who believed in Yeshua
2. The High Priest
3. He fell down to the ground
4. Yeshua
5. Saul did not eat or drink for three days

LESSON THREE: Escape from Damascus
Let's Review answers:
1. Ananias
2. Had a mikveh (special bath)
3. Yeshua
4. A group of men in Damascus
5. Saul escaped in a basket

LESSON FOUR: Saul and the disciples
Let's Review answers:
1. Saul escaped from Damascus
2. Saul had tried to arrest their friends
3. Barnabas was Saul's friend
4. Saul was brave
5. Some men did not believe that Yeshua was the Messiah

LESSON FIVE: Saul escapes Jerusalem!
Let's Review answers:
1. Jerusalem
2. They wanted to kill Paul
3. Caesarea
4. Tarsus
5. Ask children to answer this question

True or False?
Stephen was stoned to death (true)
Saul was a fireman (false)
Saul met Peter on the road to Damascus (false)
Saul escaped from Damascus (true)
Saul did not eat or drink for three days (true)
Saul lived in Egypt (false)

Discover more Activity Books!

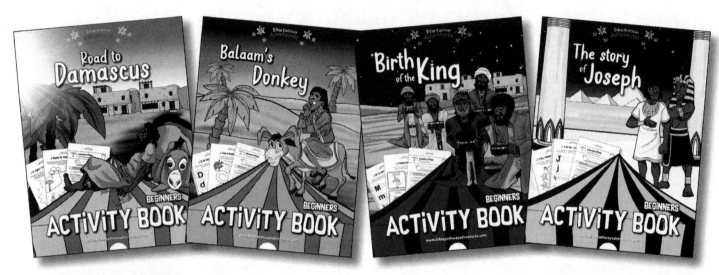

Available for purchase at www.biblepathwayadventures.com

INSTANT DOWNLOAD!

Road to Damascus	Paul's Shipwreck
Balaam's Donkey	Moses Ten Plagues
Birth of the King	The Exodus
The Story of Joseph	The Story of Esther